D1336815

This is the Third Book
by
Lynn New.

Written to warm, comfort and inspire
the many who will turn the pages
of this "Trilogy Complete."

Verses, like dreams and thoughts Fly
From the heart to roost as birds in
The Tree of Life ~
The swallow for courage,
The dove for peace,
The eagle for strength...
Read with me and let the spirit soar.

Life's Pause.

There's a time in life when we must pause,
To set aside a season, to still the world's applause.
To wonder not what might have been,
Or think of all the things we have not seen,
But stand within the shadow, the sun does cast,
And lift our eyes to God, to pray, to ask
For stillness of the heart, for peace to reign,
To take away commitment, to ease the strain.
Then when in silence standing, as rock or stone
The peace grows within us, we're not alone,
For if we can but listen, His voice we'll hear,
A whispered word of courage, in a waiting ear.
The God who dwells within us hugs a quiet place,
Always to encourage... to help us win the race.

LYNN   NEW ©

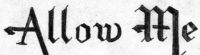

Allow Me

If I should wish to live my life and willingly
     accept the joy as well as pain,
     Allow me this, it's written in my name.
And should I dance with beggars and with kings
     it's what I must
     To see their souls, I'll dance through dusk.
And should I talk of dreams and reach for stars
     that shine so late,
     Allow me this, for this is life, I must create.
And as I walk my path, that with intent will
     twist and turn
     Let me walk unheeded for on it I shall learn.
So should my spirit fly the skies, upon it's own
     two wings,
     Allow me to accept, what e'er it brings.
If I should love and lose, yet from my heart
     find promise to forgive,
     Allow me this, for on this world we all must live.
And when the tears of laughter brim, or anguished
     drops do fall,
     Let me cry and be released; my God sees all.
And when it's time to stand against the wind
     and face reality,
     Allow me then the strength to be what I
                              must be.

LYNN NEW ©

Living in the Present.

Nothing of the past will change
It's over, done;
The Future's rather different,
It's what's to come.
The past now can not hurt you
It's memory;
The Future's more uncertain
It's what's to be.
The past can be remembered,
With ribbon tied,
But the Future Flies on wings,
Dreams undenied.
The past can be forgotten
Put out of sight,
But the Future's early dawning
Must see the light.
The past is very rigid
It will not bend,
But the Future holds the healing
To what must mend.
So think about the past
But do not dwell:
Of the Future that may scare you,
Only time will tell.
Though of one thing do be certain,
We all walk on,
And turn Future in to present
That's where we belong.

LYNN NEW ©

The Tree's Function

Take from me my life, take the saw and the knife.
Cut me till I fall away,
It's then, poor souls, I'll have my say,
For when my brothers are no more, from shore to shore
You'll look upon this barren land
And see no trees from where you stand.
No shelter in the field, for wind to yield.
No roots to hold
The soil between my fingers; my life's been sold.
Yet I who have no voice, cry out your mortal choice;
Destroy me if you must
But pay the price in barren dust.
Take my life, my lands and make your mortal plans.
Fulfil your man-made dreams,
But nothing on completion is the way it seems.
Surely man must compromise, improve his lot
yet still be wise,
And learn in his construction, to lessen great
destruction.
You need, dear friends, to realise the facts before
your very eyes;
So be aware of legacy....
when saw and chains cut down a tree.
Waste not the future of your earth
I hold great beauty and great worth.

LYNN NEW ©

The Gardener's Philosophy

He didn't seem to notice me,
He didn't see me there
I happened on the gardener
While walking deep in care.

I stood beside his garden gate
But so intent was he
He didn't glance above his work
Nor acknowledge me.

His face was caught in
winter chill,
Weathered, though serene.
His hands quite gnarled, worked
with grace
Upon all nature's scene.

He seemed quite ageless, bending
there,
The seasons turned around
And any day of any week
The gardener could be found.

I had to know the secret
Of his patient tranquil mood
But I couldn't interrupt him
Seeming to be rude.

I stood a little longer,
I watched as shadows grew
Serenity came over me
And suddenly I knew.

It wasn't what the gardener
did,
Or how he filled his time
But because he took no hurry
As I had taken mine.

He couldn't speed the pace
of growth,
Nor could he rush the seasons.
He quietly fulfilled his needs
Without preempting reasons.

If I had asked the question,
If the gardener had replied,
I'm sure he would have told me
'Don't run with life - just ride'.

LYNN NEW ©

Tonight.

Take me to your bed tonight and love me,
Let me rest within your arms and heart.
Take me to the heights from slumbered depths,
And through it all let me be a part
Of all you are and feel,
Let me know it's real.
Take me to your bed tonight
And know me.

Take me in your arms tonight, enfold me,
Caress my sleeping body till awake.
Take me from the deepest pool to wave crest,
Till I cry that it must surely break
In the rushing tide,
Nothing left to hide —
Take me in your arms again
And hold me.

Take me to your sleep tonight, protect me.
Let me share the safety of your dreams.
Take my beating heart from rush to resting,
The moment passed or so it seems.
Sleep beneath my touch
And in doing such,
Take me to your heart tonight
And love me.

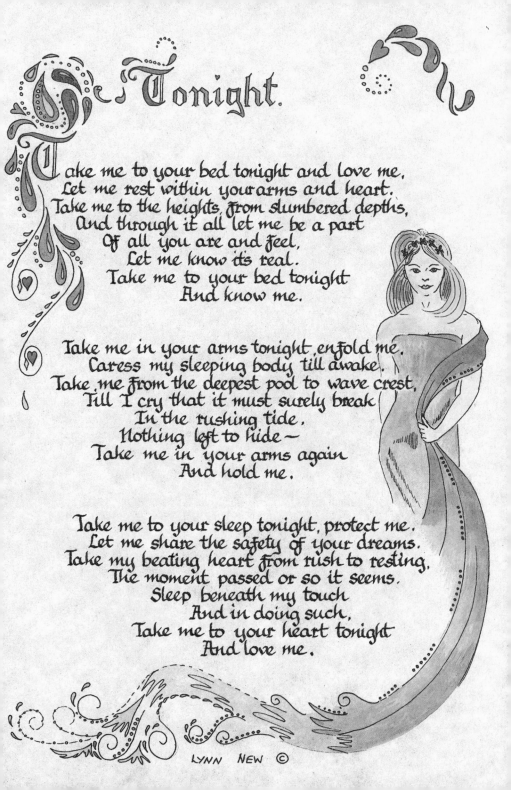

LYNN NEW ©

Sunlight.

Take the morning sun when you're awake
And let it fill your heart.
Chase the mists of dawning
It's time to make a start;
For work is never easy
There's clouds of stress and strain,
But keep the sunlight with you
And you will smile again.

Take the noon day sunshine
High above your head
And don't regret the morning
That you got out of bed,
And even if it's cloudy
Know that this is true,
Beyond the clouds of pressure
There is a sky of blue.

Take the evening sunset
At the closing of your day;
Feel the peace within you
And from inside just say,
"I'm glad the day is over,
But it's not all been bad,
The sun has shone within me
And for this I'm truly glad."

LYNN NEW ©

The Simple Daisy

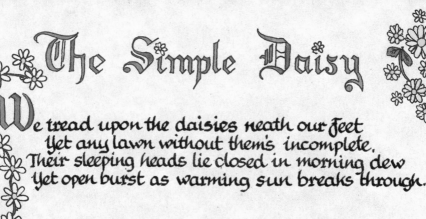

We tread upon the daisies neath our feet
　　Yet any lawn without them's incomplete.
Their sleeping heads lie closed in morning dew
Yet open burst as warming sun breaks through.

They silent grow within the grass of green,
　Taken so for granted, as they have always been.
Plucked by laughing children, time and time again,
Oh what simple pleasure gives the growing daisy chain.

As childhood fades and adolescents learn
　The art of other things, to daisies turn.
The 'love me-love me not' of petals plucked,
　Or in a button-hole, where one is kissed and tucked.

Oh, the simple daisy in the lawn,
　When mower sharply cuts 'tis ours to mourn.
　No pearl of white, or golden eye
To bless the day or praise the sky.

Yet wait, this faithful flower is strong and true.
　There's a waiting daisy already thrusting through:
　The scented rose, well painted and well versed
Matches not the daisy, the child in us loved first.

LYNN NEW ©

Taken for Granted

Don't take me for granted
I haven't come this far
To let the future slip away
To view a fading star.
Sometimes you are selfish
And can't really see
The woman, strong and silent
Who lives inside of me.
We walk that daily circle
The routine that we know,
But can you see the real me,
The part that needs to grow.

Don't take me for granted,
I'm not just a man
Who works his day in drudgery,
Earning what he can.
Sometimes you are selfish
And only see my face,
Coming home for comfort
Sitting in my place.
There is far more to me
My spirit wants to fly;
The part of me that's growing
Doesn't want to die.

Oh children, bound together
In love and earthly mould,
Spirits must be nurtured
They can't be bought or sold.
Look not within too deeply
Don't dwell too much on need,
For on the introverted
The negative does feed.
Perhaps you both feel threatened
And make your life your fight;
Acknowledge to each other
You're both of God's free Light.

LYNN NEW ©

The Eagle Within.

Some will fly on the back of an eagle
Some will flex and try their own wings,
But those who know they are destined to fly
Will hear the wind as it sings;
Will see the whole world far below them,
Will feel the sun warm their soul,
And lift as the thermals spin upward
To join, once again with the whole.

LYNN NEW ©

Life Beyond

Care for your loved one as you always have.
Let them go, but not completely.
Hold on to them, but not too tightly.
Love them as you know you will...
as you always have.
Rejoice that they are well, the only difference
now is that you can not see them,
But you feel them still and they will always
be with you.

The spirit does not die as the body dies
and Love is of the spirit.
Nothing you have experienced together can be
taken from you
And your loved one shall be eternally yours
in that love.

Weep not too long, that they may also cry,
But rejoice in their life and in yours also.
Let yours continue to be a celebration of all life;
of your shared love...
Knowing that God holds you both in the
palm of his hand
And in loving you both shall reunite you.

Blessings.

LYNN NEW ©

Universal Flame

When a candle shines in a place unknown,
It still gives light though it shines alone.
It gives a warmth, a silent prayer
Offered up to God, though no-one else is there.

When two candles burn, side by side,
Chasing out the gloom, nowhere else to hide
Multiplying strength of light, strengthening the power,
Quickening the minutes into a God-filled hour.

Then other lights attracted in universal Flame,
Gathering together in God's holy name.
Strength on strength accumulates, His power like
the sun,
So universal healing shines forth it's light as one.

LYNN NEW ©

The Sound of Spring

Listen, listen, can you hear
The surge of Spring within your ear?
Within your mind, within your heart
When Winter ends and Spring does start.

Listen, listen, blackbird's calling,
Although it seems rain won't stop falling;
It fills the ditch, the road, the garden,
Yet robin sings old nature's pardon.

Listen, listen, grass is growing,
It won't be long till it needs mowing.
But first the push through muddy verges,
Where rain and mud and silt converges.

Listen, listen, drakes are ducking,
Though when, I walk in fields I'm mucking;
And when I'm home, it's where I'm staying,
Soon come the Spring, for that I'm praying.

Listen, listen, the clouds still thunder,
And as I strain my ears, I wonder,
Do I hear Spring's first thrust to glory,
Or still to hear old Winter's story.

Listen, listen, pulses quicken,
Winter soon, in death throes stricken.
The weeks though still in early year
Call Spring time...to the listening ear.

INN NEW ©

Just to Be

If I could step aside from all that troubles me,
To stand and walk away and just to be.
If I could rise and turn my back right now
On all the cans and cants, perhaps I would learn
how
To find a peaceful spirit, a soul content,
Without explaining why, or what is meant.
If I could just let go and walk a firmer path
Away from all the pressures, yes, and the calling
hearth.
Oh that I could find the courage and learn to
say that I
Am who I want to be, my spirit wouldn't
cry.
Frustration and reality, the tearing limb from limb;
"Be calm, be still", the voice calls deeply from within.
It's time for me to love myself, to make a choice,
Not which way to turn, but to stand and hear
the voice,
Whispering a gentle strength deep inside of me,
Telling me to love myself and just
to be.

LYNN NEW ©

Peace of Mind

The other day I had a question
That I could find no answer for
So I started to ask others
Then I felt I'd know, for sure.
I needed peace and couldn't find it,
Where to look, elusive be
So I asked a man in passing,
Touched his arm and said "'cuse me".

"Peace lies up in snow-capped mountains,
Where the eagle builds her nest,
Where on climbing, you feel weary,
But you're peaceful, that's the test."
Then the woman in the market
Had a different point of view;
"When school holidays are over –
In the house there's only you!"

I walked down to the river,
Watched the angler pulling line,
"It's in the hours of waiting,
I surely do find mine."
I called a driver in the traffic
As he wound the window down –
He recoiled from the question
And his answer was a frown.

Then I jostled 'gainst a fellow
In the heaving of a crowd.
"Do you want to know what peace is?"
He called to me aloud.
"Forget about all others,
Most will search for ever more,
For peace must live within you,
Turn your own key to the door."

LYNN NEW ©

The Golden Glade.

A broken fence a thicket dense
A clinging bramble bare,
A calling bird, a calling heard
One step and I was there.

Those fallen leaves, a path deceives
A branch across my face.
My soft foot fall, I see it all
This secret, special place.

I forward bend, my path to wend
I'm breaking ground anew.
The paths divide, I must decide ~
Then suddenly I'm through.

Dark trees behind, yet now I find
I'm standing in the sun.
A clearing gold, I now behold
This place and I are one.

What magic here, what will appear
Who's watching eyes watch me?
I'm not afraid, within the glade,
For who sees I, sees me.

As if as one, the foxes run,
The rabbits to ignore,
The liquid note, from blackbirds throat
That sings old natures score.

I found I prayed within the glade
— Of which I felt a part... —
It's honoured me, that I should see
Old natures beating heart.

LYNN NEW ©

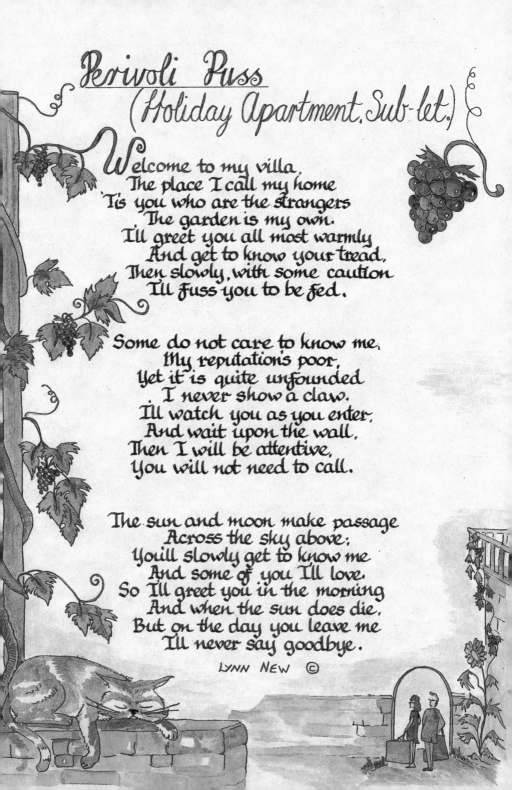

Perivoli Puss
(Holiday Apartment, Sub-let.)

Welcome to my villa,
  The place I call my home
'Tis you who are the strangers
  The garden is my own.
I'll greet you all most warmly
  And get to know your tread,
Then slowly, with some caution
  I'll Fuss you to be fed.

Some do not care to know me,
  My reputation's poor,
Yet it is quite unfounded
  I never show a claw.
I'll watch you as you enter,
  And wait upon the wall,
Then I will be attentive,
  You will not need to call.

The sun and moon make passage
  Across the sky above;
You'll slowly get to know me
  And some of you I'll love.
So I'll greet you in the morning
  And when the sun does die,
But on the day you leave me
  I'll never say goodbye.

LYNN NEW ©

Childhood Promise.

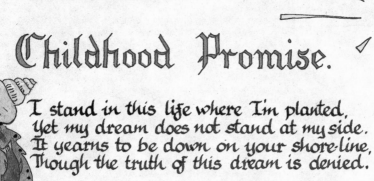

I stand in this life where I'm planted,
Yet my dream does not stand at my side.
It yearns to be down on your shore-line,
Though the truth of this dream is denied.

I sometimes hear children's voices
And carry them through in my head.
Their laughter falls all around me;
I follow on now, where I'm led.

I'm back once again in warm sunshine
Where diamonds glint on the sea,
And the gulls in the sky are harsh calling:
"I'm here, where I want to be".

And the surge of the tide over pebbles,
Like the sucking of sand from the shore,
Reminds me again of my childhood,
Unlocked now, from memories store.

Oh, the sheer wonder of rock pools,
Of cobbos and small fish at play.
The bucket of crabs to return to
The sea, at the end of the day.

But most, I remember the promise
I made and to which I am bound,
If in life I must stay where I'm planted
In my dreams, this is where I'll be found.

LYNN NEW ©

He Calls The Tune.

I hear the tune of life so clear,
The whispered breeze, distant - but near.
Let God compose His symphony
Of natures sounds I can not see.

The Master calls the pipes that play
Within the year that runs its day.
The autumn leaves that brittle fall
At some command, or hidden call.

And coming forth from natures throat
The creaking trees plain single note.
The grinding of old wood on wood
That's weathered all from where its stood.

The Flutist's note within the stream
Wafts to me as I silent dream;
And as the water hurries by
It's joined by sedges whispered sigh.

Last days, the sun in silent glory
Sheds now its light on autumns story,
And though it utters not a sound
It stirs a mouse from underground.

The drum that sounds the autumn beat
Once called all nature to its feet.
It quickened for the spring to follow
The winter frost within woods hollow.

And as God's world winds down to rest
I feel a stirring in my breast,
For always will Lifes music play
Through seasons own melodious way.

LYNN NEW ©

The Celebration of Birth.

"I am old", said the world, "but I welcome
and celebrate the arrival of each precious
child, who are souls in their own right.
— To them I bring eternal gifts :-

I bring light that they may see their way
    And shelter that they may rest.
Air to breathe and rain for refreshment.
To each I give a family to love
                            and be loved by.
All this I give and more. Gifts that they will
search for and find throughout their lives;
    that will bring peace and harmony and
    lighten the days and fill their spirits.

Each child is a treasure, beyond weight or
measure, priceless and unique. For there are
no two alike — to cry the same, nor demand
the same from me. Each is an individual,
with their own spark of creation — brought
in love, to their families, to be nurtured and
cultivated as seeds, to become as flowers in
my garden.

In return for the gifts I freely bestowed
at their birth they in turn shall honour
me with their own gifts—
    The greatest of these being Love."

And the old world, in his wisdom, spoke for
    all those who gather to celebrate the miracle
    of birth and creation in the knowledge that
    babes and growing children are already
        brave, strong spirits
            in the making —

LYNN NEW ©

Retirement

So now you're retiring and can hang up your coat,
You can watch from the window
Or stand there and gloat,
At all other souls going to work
And know it is something you never did shirk.

They call it retirement, for want of a name,
And yet, so they tell me
Your life starts again.
It holds the promise of dreams in your head
Which gave you incentive to get out of bed.

Life will pass slowly, that's what people say,
You can do what you fancy...
Be lazy all day.
But life has a habit of laughing at you,
There's no time at all to do things you want to.

So much there to see, to do and to say,
For time moves more quickly
Than ever, each day.
So think of your friends you're leaving behind
And all the new "hobbies" you'll surely find.

LYNN NEW ©

Trottered Truth!

It isn't very fair to say
A pig's a pig in every way.
They can be brown or cream or pink,
It isn't fair to say they stink.
It's said, they snort and squeal, that's true.
If, I were prodded I would too.
They're fat and slow, with trottered feet,
Some say they're only good to eat,
And yet, you know, these folk offend.
There's many a pig, who needs a friend....
Many a pig who's better than they.
Despite the insults hurled his way.
So when you see a pig, don't sneer...
To another pig, a pig is dear!

LYNN NEW ©

Belated

Better late than never
That's what they all say
But I didn't want to let you down
And miss the special day.
Perhaps my mind was too full
Of all I had to do
But it was my full intention
To get in touch with you.
I'm feeling rather guilty
You may think I didn't care
No card pushed through the letter box
Or friendly word to share.
I'm hoping that it went well
And the day was just as planned
And when you read this ditty
You will understand
That "it's better late than never"
These words will still hold true.
I may have missed that special date
But I'd not forgotten you.

LYNN NEW ©

The Parting Gift

I could not walk your path, my friend,
   I had to walk my own.
I had to plant my footsteps
   On a path already shown.
I did not have a choice, my friend
   I knew I could not stay;
I had to leave your bordered path,
   I had to find my way.
Your path for me was easy,
   I could have stumbled on,
But something deep inside of me
   Knew that it was wrong.
I could not walk behind you,
   In front, nor by your side,
I had to step out bravely
   My path was not that wide.
And neither could I wait for you
   Though surely did I try;
I didn't know the reason,
   I could not tell you why.
But now it's done, we've parted,
   The past is left behind.
My path leads to fulfilment
   And peace, I hope to find.
Now as dear friends we'll travel
   Our paths may often cross,
And slowly life will kindle
   From the ashes of our loss.
Be brave, my love, look not behind,
   Face front, you will not fall.
In giving me my freedom
   You've given me —
     my all!

LYNN NEW ©

Congratulations

The word congratulations
Portrays so many things
But in every case there's heart felt joy
That celebration brings
And this is one occasion where congratulation's due
For all the folk who've heard your news
Are very proud of you.
Perhaps there'll be a party
To mark the great event
While cards and gifts may shower you,
From every corner sent.
Folk will want to shake your hand
While others hug and kiss
But no matter what goes on today
Just remember this...
The reason that you celebrate
Should not go ignored
But you have made it possible
So its you we now applaud.

Congratulation

LYNN NEW ©

Questions

And what of I, who beats with everlasting life...
   And what of I?
   Have I not too a dream I can't deny?
Have I not wings to beat, a voice to sing?
   Ah, little world, and what of I?

And who am I, whose very life is made of love...
   And who am I?
   Is there not an urgent call, a need to Fly?
Have I not wings upon my feet, though earthly shod?
   Ah, clay made world, but who am I?

And why am I, whose visioned eyes were meant to see...
   Why am I?
Have I not life to call my own, before I die?
And would it not be sacrilege to let it waste away?
   Oh, dying world, so why am I?

And how shall I, who ponders now upon the ground...
   But how shall I?
Will courage raise my eyes and blaze the sky
   with spirit brave and fearless quiet heart?
   Oh, anguished world, but how shall I?

It's now that I shall count the blessings that I hold...
   It's now that I
Shall let the talents I possess, grow wings to Fly:
Blown on the winds of life, dark corners given light.
   Ah, needy world, you shall know I.

LYNN NEW   ©

Await the Calm

Take courage, stand still and be strong
The wind and the rain shall not
            hurt you
    And all that you silently bear
Will not hurt, or destroy, only shake you

Time soon for the storm to subside,
  May calmness abound and console you;
  Then sunlight from shadows emerge
  To warm and uplift an enfold you:

LYNN NEW ©

Gods Holy House

Oh hallowed place of holy ways,
That rises to the vaulted roof before my very gaze.
That makes me lift my eyes to heavens stair
And welcomes me and bids me there.

Oh hallowed place and holy seat
Whose flooring flags lie worn neath my feet.
Once told the monologue of families great
Now only fine inscriptions do relate.

Oh hallowed place and holy shell
Whose columns great, of single strength, stand well.
And silently bear witness from their post
And hold the ceiling high, for man and Holy Ghost.

Ah, hallowed place and shelter mine
Whose pews in reverence, like regimental soldiers line,
Lead my eyes beyond to rest my gaze
From aisle to the altar, where shafting sunlight lays.

Ah hallowed place, a perfect start
For prayers from bended knee to fly from heart.
And candles light the way in symbolic right
To raise the word confirming now God's healing light.

Ah hallowed place where whispers heard
Whose windows stained with love and glory of his word.
Each colour, piece and prism, exalt the story told
Born of light in lead, from framing walls enfold.

Ah hallowed place, my God does call
Let me leave, at length, when I have seen it all,
Not with my eyes, though they have had their fill
But with my spirits vision of God's Holy will.

LYNN NEW ©

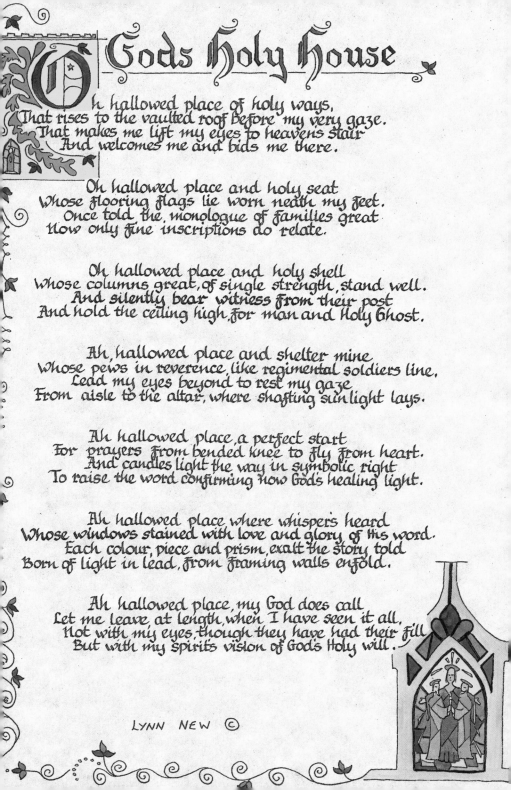

Town & Country

Said the town to the country "I'm restless and growing
I want more houses where your farmers are sowing.
I need more space, for my people are squeezing
And when you breathe air ~ I'm coughing and sneezing."

But the country looked on at the town in it's pity,
And saw that quite soon it would grow to a city;
Already roads crossed without even asking
Gone soon would be badger and butterfly basking.

"I'm sorry, old town, with your fingers of progress,
If I give you more, it is I who will have less,
And then I will be weak and you'll be much stronger
Soon to be noticed that I am no longer."

"So what shall I do if you don't accept me,
Noise and pollution will start to affect me?
If you give me your land, it will ease the pressure;
You don't need it all ~ you use some for leisure."

So the fields and the hills and the rivers a running
All clubbed together to stop the town coming.
Parliament passed a law that by order
Would limit progression beyond the green border.

Now the town and the country, side by side they were living
The battle was won, of the taking and giving.
But cars in their hundreds are coming and going
Destroying the country without even knowing.   LYNN NEW ©

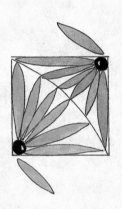

A Mother's Grief.

Why should it be? We often ask.
  Why did it happen so?
What is the reason behind it,
  Why did my child go?

What about all the others,
  Those who cause worry and pain?
Those who care not and are greedy,
Doing evil for what they will gain.

Who made the fateful decision?
  I see no reason or rhyme.
Why did you take my dear child?
  I know that it wasn't the time.

Be patient, dear mother, I'll tell you,
  It's natural to feel this way.
Your desolate anger rides forward
  For you see not your child at play.

But this story is not really over,
  New life in full glory's begun,
Your child, on earth knew its shadows
  Now stands in the warmth with
        my Son.

Take heart and let no-one tell you
  That time will heal your pain,
It will often walk on beside you
Till you laugh with your child again.

LYNN NEW ©

Direction.

I stood before a scene unveiled
Yet never knew what it entailed,
For here I am, yet not by chance,
I am part too, of spirit's dance.

Who brought me to this place in time,
This place that now my heart calls mine?
Who led me by the hand and said,
"By manna only, you'll be fed"?

Who brushed my tears and kissed them dry?
Who knew there was a time to cry;
Who told me not where, I should go,
But every step confirmed it so?

Who whispered low, in silent voice,
"You have a choice—and yet no choice";
Who also stood behind my back
Should I turn round, in moments lack?

And so, I stand and now I see,
The mission's here~it's inside me.
If I can trust that unseen hand
I'll know, in time, what God has planned.

LYNN NEW ©

The Sum of Love

L
O
V
E

$$\frac{2}{4}$$

$5 + 5 = 10$

$1 + 1 = 2$

MULTIPLY ME & YOU = 2

Let's say love is the equation
Made up of many things,
The adding and subtracting
That understanding brings.

You've taken all my worries
And divided them by two,
I've seen the shadows roll away
And then the sun shone through.

And when in rich contentment
You let your hand hold mine,
It's not only our ten fingers
But our two hearts entwine.

So as you add your life to mine
You'll know that it is true,
For just as love's the answer
The sum of it is you.

LYNN NEW ©

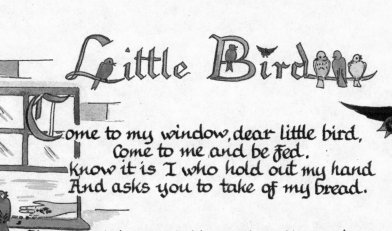

Little Bird

Come to my window, dear little bird,
Come to me and be fed.
Know it is I who hold out my hand
And asks you to take of my bread.

Stand not by the table and wait for the crust
That falls from another bird's beak,
But wait by my door, with patience, sweet bird,
I'll give you what surely you seek.

How hopeful you gaze at the table above
And wait till the crumbs fall to ground:
But, little bird, surely you know,
From me, all your food may be found.

So why, little bird, of hunger and hope
Do you feed from what's dropped from above?
You'll only receive what you've come to expect
But from me you will receive love.

So tarry no longer than you surely must,
Crumbs also stop falling in time.
You're worth so much more than another's crust,
But all that I have shall be thine.

LYNN NEW ©

Giving Thanks .

Thank you God, for giving me
Two perfect eyes that I may see;
Two ears to hear
Two lips to speak,
A will to search for things I seek.

Thankyou Friends for being there
With all your joy and time to spare.
For judging not
Yet missing me,
When on your doorstep I can't be.

Thankyou birds of cheerful voice
And for a spirit giving choice
In all I do
If I have mind,
I'm grateful that I'm not confined.

And if in time, when I grow old
And have no choice and must be told
Read me these words
To realise
I am still useful, in God's eyes.

LYNN NEW ©

The End of the Beginning

As the eyes that scan the page of printed word
  See the poem from my soul so newly heard,
So the lines run free, like flowing flag unfurled.
Words like these are written with hope to heal the world.
  For if in any verse that's read, you recollect
Something of yourself and makes some marked effect
    I too will know achievement of my own
    For what are words if they can not be thrown
        From the heart into a waiting pond
That ripples, reaching outward as each of you respond,
For hidden in each poem is the seed of your own thought
And if you recognize just some, closer you've been
                        brought
    To the peaceful spirit dwelling in your heart....
        Make not this verse the ending....
          ...but make it just the start.

LYNN NEW ©